BritBound:
A Guide for Asian Wives in the U.K.

Arthur Crandon LL.B. (Hons.) M.A.

BritBound:

A Guide for Asian Wives in the U.K.

Copyright Arthur Crandon 2024

All rights reserved. No part of this book may be reproduced, stored in a retrieval system, or transmitted in any form or by any means—electronic, mechanical, photocopying, recording, or otherwise—without the prior written permission of the publisher, except for brief quotations in critical reviews or articles.

This is a work of fiction. Names, characters, places, and incidents are either the product of the author's imagination or used fictitiously. Any resemblance to actual persons, living or dead, events, or locales is entirely coincidental.

ISBN: 9798342093026

Cover design by Lynnie Ceniza
Interior design and formatting by Lynnie Ceniza
Published by Arthur Crandon Publishing
Visit our website: Arthurcrandon.co.uk

DISCLAIMER

The information provided in this book is for general informational purposes only. It does not constitute legal, financial, or professional advice. While every effort has been made to ensure accuracy, the author and publisher assume no responsibility for errors or omissions. Readers should consult with appropriate professionals for specific advice tailored to their individual circumstances.

First Edition: August 2024

"THE MELTING POT":

THE UK IS A VIBRANT TAPESTRY OF CULTURES. FROM SIPPING TEA IN COZY CAFÉS TO EXPLORING HISTORIC CASTLES, YOU'LL FIND SOMETHING FOR EVERY TASTE. BUT BRACE YOURSELF FOR THE WEATHER—IT'S A MOODY COMPANION. RAIN OR SHINE, THE LUSH GREEN COUNTRYSIDE AND BUSTLING CITY LIFE AWAIT. JUST MIND THE GAP ON THE TUBE, AND DON'T FORGET TO INDULGE IN FISH AND CHIPS!

CONTENTS

	Acknowledgments	i
1	Summary	1
2	Cultural Differences	9
3	Legal	13
4	Language	15
5	Jobs and Careers	21
6	Education	35
7	Culture and Food	43
8	Emotional Reisilience	49
9	Driving and Transport	57
10	Finance and Benefits	65

"NAVIGATING THE ETIQUETTE DANCE":

IN THE UK, POLITENESS REIGNS SUPREME. QUEUES (LINES) ARE SACRED—NEVER JUMP AHEAD! LEARN THE ART OF SMALL TALK ABOUT THE WEATHER (IT'S PRACTICALLY A NATIONAL SPORT). AND WHEN INVITED FOR A CUPPA, SAY YES—EVEN IF YOU'RE A COFFEE LOVER. EMBRACE THE ECCENTRICITIES, FROM DOUBLE-DECKER BUSES TO CRICKET MATCHES. CHEERS, MATE!

1 SUMMARY

Thousands of Asian wives of UK men arrive here every year. Mainly from Philippines and Thailand, but also from China, Indonesia, Cambodia and Vietnam. It can be a very big culture shock.
We wish to help them to adapt.

Adapting to life in the UK as an Asian wife involves a mix of practical adjustments, cultural awareness, and emotional resilience. Here's a comprehensive list of strategies and considerations:

1. **Understanding Cultural Differences:**

    - **Learn About British Culture:**
        - Familiarize yourself with British customs, traditions, and social norms.

Understand the British sense of humor, communication style, and etiquette.
- Be open-minded and curious about local practices.

2. **Legal and Practical Matters:**

    o **Visa and Immigration:**
        - Understand your visa status and any associated restrictions.
        - Keep track of visa expiration dates and renewal requirements.

    o **Healthcare Registration:**
        - Register with a local doctor (GP) to access healthcare services.
        - Learn about the National Health Service (NHS) and how it works.

3. **Language and Communication:**

    o **Improve English Language Skills:**
        - Take English language classes if needed.

- Practice speaking with native speakers to build confidence.

- **Local Slang and Expressions:**
  - Learn common British phrases and slang to enhance communication.

4. **Social Integration:**

   - **Join Community Groups:**
     - Attend local events, community centers, and cultural gatherings.
     - Connect with other Asian expatriates and locals.

   - **Volunteer or Join Clubs:**
     - Participate in volunteering activities or join clubs related to your interests.
     - Engage in hobbies or sports to meet like-minded people.

5. **Work and Career:**

   - **Job Search:**
     - Update your CV (resume) to match UK standards.

- Explore job opportunities in your field.

- **Networking:**
  - Attend industry events, conferences, and networking sessions.
  - Connect with professionals in your sector.

6. **Family and Relationships:**

   - **Support System:**
     - Maintain communication with family back home.
     - Build a local support network through friends, neighbors, and community members.

   - **Childcare and Education:**
     - Research local schools and educational options for your children.
     - Understand the UK education system.

7. **Cultural Adaptation:**

   - **Food and Cuisine:**
     - Explore British cuisine while

    also enjoying your own traditional dishes.
  - Try local foods and visit multicultural markets.

- **Weather and Dress Code:**
  - Prepare for the UK's unpredictable weather. Invest in warm clothing and waterproof gear.
  - Adapt your wardrobe to suit different seasons.

8. **Emotional Resilience:**

   - **Homesickness:**
     - Acknowledge feelings of homesickness and find healthy ways to cope.
     - Stay connected with loved ones through video calls and visits.

   - **Cultural Identity:**
     - Embrace your cultural heritage while appreciating the diversity around you.
     - Seek out cultural events and

festivals.

9. **Driving and Transportation:**

    - **Driving License:**
        - If you plan to drive, apply for a UK driving license.
        - Learn about road rules and traffic signs.

    - **Public Transport:**
        - Familiarize yourself with local buses, trains, and underground systems.

10. **Financial Literacy:**

    - **Banking and Taxes:**
        - Open a UK bank account.
        - Understand tax regulations and filing requirements.

Remember that adaptation takes time, and it's okay to feel overwhelmed initially. Be patient with yourself, seek support when needed, and celebrate the small victories along the way. You're embarking on a unique and enriching journey!

2 CULTURAL DIFFERENCES

Understanding cultural differences is essential for a smooth transition when adapting to life in the UK as an Asian wife. Let's delve into some key aspects:

1. **Politeness and Respect:**
    - British women are often known for their polite demeanor, which can sometimes be mistaken for aloofness. However, it's a sign of respect.
    - Appreciate this cultural trait and respond with equal courtesy.

2. **British Humor:**
   - British social interactions thrive on wit and dry humor.
   - Participate in banter, appreciate clever comments, and don't take everything too seriously.

3. **Independence:**
   - Many British women value their independence—both financially and emotionally.
   - Recognize and appreciate their individuality.

4. **Dating Nuances:**

   - **Subtle Flirting:**
     - Overt gestures may not be well-received. Clever comments and paying attention matter more.

   - **Tea Time Ritual:**
     - It's not just a drink; it's an opportunity for intimate conversations.

- **Shared Understanding:**
    - Little moments of connection matter—whether it's a shared laugh or a genuine conversation.

Remember, it's about more than just dating; it's about building lasting connections. Embrace the nuances, enjoy the journey, and appreciate the quintessential British experience!

3 LEGAL

When it comes to legal and practical matters for Asian wives adapting to life in the UK, there are a few key steps to consider:

1. **Visa and Immigration:**

    o **Understand Your Visa Status:**
        - Familiarize yourself with the terms of your visa. Know any associated restrictions.
        - Keep track of visa expiration dates and renewal requirements.

2. **Healthcare Registration:**

    o **Register with a Local Doctor (GP):**

        - Accessing healthcare services in the UK starts with registering at a GP surgery (general practitioner's office).
        - You don't need proof of address or immigration status to register.

    o **Learn About the National Health Service (NHS):**

        - The NHS provides healthcare services in the UK.
        - Understand how it works, including emergency care, prescriptions, and specialist referrals.

Remember, these practical steps ensure you're well-prepared for your new life in the UK.

4 LANGUAGE

When it comes to improving English language skills and understanding local slang and expressions in the UK, here are some practical steps for Asian wives:

1. **English Language Classes:**
    - Consider enrolling in English language courses. These classes cater to various proficiency levels and can help you enhance your reading, writing, speaking, and listening skills.
    - Look for accredited language schools or centers approved by the UK Government and education authorities.

2. **Practice with Native Speakers:**
   - Engage in conversations with native English speakers. Practice speaking, ask questions, and actively listen.
   - Join language exchange groups or find language partners online.

3. **Learn British Slang and Expressions:**
   - British slang adds color and authenticity to your language skills. Explore common phrases and idiomatic expressions used in everyday conversations.
   - Familiarize yourself with terms like "bloke," "knackered," "gutted," "gobsmacked," and "chuffed."

Remember, language learning is an exciting journey, and embracing local expressions will make your interactions more engaging and enjoyable!

! Improving your spoken English by practicing with native speakers is a fantastic way to enhance your language skills. Here are several effective ways to practice speaking with native English speakers:

1. **Online Language Exchange Platforms:**

- **Cambly**: Cambly connects you with native English speakers for one-on-one video chat sessions. You can discuss various topics, receive real-time feedback, and improve your fluency.

- **Preply**: On Preply, you can find native-speaking English tutors who offer personalized lessons. Book online sessions and engage in conversations to enhance your speaking skills.

2. **Join Conversation Groups or Clubs:**

    - Look for local or online conversation groups where native speakers gather to discuss various topics. These groups often meet in person or virtually.
    - Attend language exchange events, meetups, or workshops. Engage in casual conversations and learn from each other.

3. **Language Apps and Websites:**

    o **Tandem**: Tandem is an app that connects language learners with native speakers. You can chat via text, voice, or video calls.

    o **HelloTalk**: HelloTalk allows you to chat with native speakers through text messages, voice recordings, and even video calls.

4. **Watch English Content with Subtitles**

    o Choose movies, TV shows, or YouTube videos in English. Turn on subtitles to follow along.
    o Pay attention to pronunciation, intonation, and natural speech patterns.

5. **Record Yourself Speaking:**
    o Use your smartphone or a voice recorder app to record yourself speaking in English.
    o Listen to the recordings and identify areas for improvement.

6. **Practice Pronunciation and Intonation:**

    - Mimic native speakers. Pay attention to how they stress certain words and phrases.
    - Focus on linking words together (e.g., contractions) and using natural intonation.

7. **Join Online Language Challenges:**
    - Some websites and social media platforms host language challenges. For example, the "1000 Native English Conversations" video on YouTube offers exposure to various accents and phrases.

Remember, consistency is key. Set aside dedicated time each day to practice speaking with native speakers. Be open to making mistakes—it's all part of the learning process!

5 JOBS AND CAREERS

Let's dive into each of these steps to help you enhance your job search and career prospects:

1. **Updating Your CV (Resume) to Match UK Standards**: Keeping your CV up-to-date is crucial, whether you're actively job searching or content in your current role. Here are some steps to ensure your CV reflects your skills and experiences effectively:

    o **Research and Optimize**: Large companies often use applicant tracking systems (ATS) to scan CVs for specific keywords. Research job descriptions and advertisements related to your desired position. Identify common keywords and incorporate them into your CV. Also, explore professional networking sites to understand the skills and qualifications valued in your chosen career.

- **Refresh Your Summary or Objective**: Your CV summary provides a brief overview of your key skills and experiences. Make sure it reflects your most recent and relevant qualities. Consider incorporating new skills and experiences you've gained. If your objective statement is outdated, consider using a concise CV summary instead.

- **Remove Outdated Information**: As you add new information, remove outdated details. Eliminate old jobs that aren't relevant to your target position. For instance, you might remove high school achievements and focus on degree-level qualifications as you progress in your career,

- **Highlight Achievements**: While summarizing your duties is essential, focus on showcasing your achievements. Recruiters want to know what additional value you can bring to a role. Highlight specific accomplishments that set you apart from other candidates.

If you'd like more detailed guidance, websites like Indeed and VisualCV offer comprehensive guides on updating your CV to UK standards'

2. **Exploring Job Opportunities in Your Field**: To explore job opportunities effectively, consider the following steps:

    - **Start with Self-Reflection**: Think about your interests, what motivates you, and responsibilities you excelled at in school or previous jobs. Make a list of what's important to you in a career and the industries or causes that resonate with you.

    - **Research Viable Careers**: Based on your interests, research careers that align with your criteria. Look into job descriptions, salaries, required education, and daily tasks. Consider taking free online career assessments to identify suitable career paths.

- **Attend Industry-Specific Networking Events**: These events allow you to connect with peers and industry experts. You'll learn about industry trends, expand your knowledge, and potentially discover new career opportunities. Seminars and conferences are excellent places to network.

- **Use Social Media and Local Calendars**: Platforms like Twitter, Facebook, and industry-specific websites can help you find relevant job openings. Join relevant industry groups and stay informed about events and opportunities.

3. **Networking at Industry Events and Conferences**: Networking is essential for career growth. Here are some types of networking events you might consider:

- **Industry-Specific Networking Events**: Attend seminars and conferences related to your field. These events provide valuable connections and keep you informed about industry developments.

- **Happy Hour Networking Events**: These casual gatherings allow you to mingle with professionals in a relaxed setting. They're great for meeting local peers and initiating conversations.

- **Professional Conferences**: Look out for conferences specific to your industry. They offer opportunities to learn, connect, and stay updated on trends.

- **Alumni Networking Events**: Connect with fellow alumni from your educational institution. Alumni networks often organize events where you can meet professionals from various fields[1].

Remember, networking isn't just about handing out business cards—it's about building genuine relationships. Be curious, ask questions, and listen actively. You never know where a valuable connection might lead!

Networking is a powerful tool for career growth, and it doesn't have to be intimidating. Let's explore some practical tips to help you network effectively:

1. **Talk to New People at Networking Events**:

    - When attending networking events, make the most of your time by meeting as many new people as possible. Approach others with a friendly smile and engage in genuine conversations. Remember, networking isn't just about exchanging business cards; it's about building relationships.

2. **Attend New Events**:

    - Don't limit yourself to the same circles. Explore different types of events—industry-specific conferences, workshops, meetups, and even social gatherings. Each event offers unique opportunities to connect with diverse professionals.
    -

3. **Create Authentic Relationships**:

    o Instead of focusing solely on what you can gain, think about how you can contribute to the relationship. Be genuinely interested in others. Ask about their work, interests, and experiences. Authentic connections are more valuable than superficial ones.

4. **Bring a Memorable Business Card**:

    o While digital networking is essential, having a well-designed business card can leave a lasting impression. Include relevant information (name, contact details, LinkedIn profile) and a brief tagline that reflects your expertise or passion.

5. **Be Confident**:

    o Confidence matters! Stand tall, maintain eye contact, and introduce yourself with clarity. Remember that everyone at a networking event is there for the same purpose—to connect and learn from one another.

6. **Stay Connected**:

    o   After meeting someone, follow up promptly. Connect on LinkedIn, send a personalized message, and express your interest in continuing the conversation. Regularly engage with your network by sharing relevant content or attending follow-up events[1].

7. **Help Others in Your Network**:

    o   Networking isn't just about what you can get; it's also about what you can give. Offer assistance, share knowledge, and introduce people within your network. Helping others strengthens relationships and builds trust.

8. **Revisit Older Connections**:

    o   Don't forget about existing contacts. Reach out to former colleagues, mentors, or classmates. Rekindle those relationships—they might lead to unexpected opportunities[1].

Remember, networking is about building meaningful connections, not collecting business cards. Be curious, listen actively, and be open to learning from others.

Networking online can be just as impactful as in-person networking, and it's especially relevant in today's interconnected world. Whether you're looking to expand your professional circle, explore job opportunities, or simply connect with like-minded individuals, here are some tips to help you network effectively online:

1. **Optimize Your Online Profiles**:

    o **Update Your Profiles**: Before diving into online networking, ensure your profiles on platforms like LinkedIn, Twitter, or professional forums are up-to-date. Use a professional photo, write a compelling summary, and highlight your skills and experiences.

2. **Know Your Goals**:

    o **Define Your Objectives**: Consider what you want to achieve through networking. Are you looking for job leads, industry insights, or mentorship? Knowing your goals will guide your networking efforts.

3. **Balance Your Network**:

   - **Diverse Connections**: Aim for a balanced network. Connect with people from various backgrounds, industries, and roles. Diversity enriches your network and exposes you to different perspectives.

4. **Personalize Your Messages**:

   - **Skip Generic Messages**: When reaching out to someone, avoid generic messages. Instead, personalize your introductions. Mention common interests, shared connections, or specific reasons for connecting.

5. **Participate Actively**:

   - **Join Online Communities**: Engage in relevant groups, forums, and social media communities. Participate in discussions, share insights, and contribute valuable content. Consistent activity helps you build credibility and visibility.

6. **Stay Informed**:

    o **Know Industry Trends**: Regularly read industry news, blogs, and reports. Being well-informed allows you to contribute meaningfully to conversations and positions you as a knowledgeable networker.

7. **Help Others**:

    o **Give Before You Receive**: Networking isn't just about taking; it's about giving. Offer assistance, share resources, and connect people within your network. Generosity fosters stronger relationships.

8. **Connect Early and Often**:

    o **Consistent Interaction**: Don't wait until you need something to connect. Regularly check in with your network—comment on their posts, congratulate them on achievements, and maintain a genuine presence.

9. **Choose the Right Platforms**:

    o **LinkedIn**: For professional networking, LinkedIn is essential. Connect with colleagues, industry peers, and potential employers. Join relevant groups and participate in discussions.

    o **Twitter**: Follow industry influencers, participate in Twitter chats, and share valuable content. Twitter is excellent for real-time conversations.

    o **Industry-Specific Forums**: Explore forums related to your field. These niche communities allow you to connect with like-minded professionals.

10. **Attend Virtual Events**:

    o **Webinars, Conferences, and Workshops**: Many events have moved online. Attend webinars, virtual conferences, and workshops. Use the chat features to engage with speakers and other attendees.

11. **Be Authentic and Approachable**:

    - **Be Yourself**: Authenticity matters. Be genuine, share your experiences, and express your passion for your field. People appreciate authenticity over rehearsed networking pitches.

Remember, online networking is about building meaningful relationships, not just accumulating connections.

6 EDUCATION

Let's dive into understanding the UK education system, especially when it comes to children.

In the United Kingdom, education is organized into several stages, ensuring a comprehensive learning journey for young ones. Here's a breakdown:

1. **Early Years (Preschool and Reception)**:
    - Children typically start their formal education at around 5 years old (4 in Northern Ireland).
    - The early years focus on building foundational skills, including language, communication, literacy,

and basic math.
- Teachers assess pupils' starting points during this stage.

2. **Primary Education (Key Stages 1 and 2)**:
   - Key Stage 1 (KS1): Ages 5 to 7
     - Children continue to develop literacy, numeracy, and other essential skills.
     - The Phonics screening check takes place during Year 1.
   - Key Stage 2 (KS2): Ages 7 to 11
     - National tests in English reading and math occur in Year 2.
     - Teacher assessments cover math, science, and English reading and writing in Year 2.
     - Year 6 sees national tests in English reading, math, and grammar, punctuation, and spelling. Teacher assessments also include English writing and science.

3. **Secondary Education (Key Stages 3 and 4)**:
   - Key Stage 3 (KS3): Ages 11 to 14
     - Students continue their studies, exploring a wider

range of subjects.
- Key Stage 4 (KS4): Ages 14 to 16
  - Most children take their GCSEs (General Certificate of Secondary Education) during this stage.
  - GCSEs cover various subjects and serve as important qualifications for further education or employment.

4. **Further Education (FE)**:
   - After completing compulsory education, students can pursue further education.
   - FE includes A-Levels, GNVQs (General National Vocational Qualifications), BTECs (Business and Technology Education Council), and other qualifications.
   - FE institutions provide specialized courses and training.

5. **Higher Education (HE)**:
   - Beyond secondary education, students can attend universities or colleges for higher education.
   - HE offers undergraduate and postgraduate degrees in various fields.

Remember that the English national curriculum ensures that children in different schools (both primary and secondary) study the same subjects to similar standards. It's a well-structured system that aims to provide a solid foundation for lifelong learning!

Choosing the right school for your child is an important decision, and I'm here to guide you through it! Here are some steps to help you make an informed choice:

1. **Types of Schools**:
    - Understand the different types of schools available in the UK. These include state-funded schools (such as community schools, academies, and free schools) and private/independent schools. Each type has its own features and benefits[1].
    - Consider whether you want your child to attend a state-funded school or explore private options.

2. **Location and Accessibility**:

- Think about proximity. How close is the school to your home? Shorter commutes can make life easier for both you and your child.
- Consider transportation options, such as school buses or walking routes.

3. **Curriculum**:
   - Research the curriculum offered by the school. Does it align with your educational preferences? Some schools follow traditional curricula, while others may have specialized programs (e.g., Montessori, International Baccalaureate).
   - Look into subjects taught, teaching methods, and extracurricular opportunities.

4. **Academic Performance and Ofsted Ratings**:
   - Check the school's academic track record. Look at exam results, progression rates, and overall performance.
   - Visit the school's most recent Ofsted reports. These provide insights into teaching quality, student well-being, and leadership.

5. **Special Educational Needs (SEN)**:
    - If your child has specific needs, investigate how the school supports SEN students. Are there dedicated resources, trained staff, and individualized plans?
    - Reach out to the school to discuss any specific requirements your child may have.

6. **Extracurricular Activities**:
    - Consider what the school offers beyond academics. Are there clubs, sports teams, music programs, or art classes?
    - Extracurricular activities contribute to a well-rounded education and can enhance your child's social skills.

7. **School Culture and Values**:
    - Visit potential schools and meet with staff. Get a feel for the atmosphere. Is it nurturing, inclusive, and supportive?
    - Talk to other parents about their experiences. Their insights can be

invaluable.

8. **Fees and Scholarships (for Private Schools)**:
    - If you're considering a private school, understand the fees and any available scholarships.
    - Some private schools offer financial aid or scholarships based on merit or need.

Remember, every child is unique, so consider your child's individual needs, interests, and personality when making your decision. And don't hesitate to visit schools, ask questions, and gather as much information as possible. You're doing great by researching and planning ahead!

7 CULTURE AND FOOD

Let's dive into cultural adaptation, both in terms of food and dressing for the UK.

Exploring British Cuisine:
When it comes to food, the United Kingdom offers a delightful blend of tradition, innovation, and multicultural influences. Let's take a culinary tour:

1. **Traditional British Dishes**:

    o **Fish and Chips**: A quintessential British classic! Imagine crispy battered fish served alongside

golden chips (that's fries to our American friends). Don't forget the mushy peas—a delightful addition.
- **Roast Beef with Yorkshire Pudding**: Sunday lunch perfection! Slow-cooked roast beef paired with a light, airy Yorkshire pudding. Add roasted veggies like carrots and Brussels sprouts for the full experience.
- **Full English Breakfast**: A hearty morning feast featuring bacon, eggs, sausages, grilled tomatoes, mushrooms, and toast. It's the ultimate weekend indulgence.

2. **Must-Try Ingredients**:

   - **Rozanne Apples**: These sweet and crunchy apples are native to the UK. Perfect for snacking or pairing with savory dishes like pork chops and apple sauce.

3. **Multicultural Influence**:
   - The UK's food scene isn't just about traditional fare. It's a melting pot of flavors! Explore international delights—Indian curries, Middle Eastern kebabs, Thai noodles, and

more. You'll find global cuisines readily available in cities like London.

Dressing for the British Weather:

Ah, the ever-changing British climate! Here's how to stay stylishly prepared:

1. **Layers, Layers, Layers**:
    - Think of layers as your secret weapon against unpredictable skies. Start with lightweight tees (for unexpected warmth) and add snug fleece or wool layers that can be bundled up.
    - A versatile sweater is your best friend—it's chic and practical when the temperature dips.

2. **Footwear Matters**:
    - Navigating historic streets and green parks demands reliable shoes. Look for good support and grip. Remember, it's not just about waterproofing; breathable shoes keep your feet dry from within.
    - For upscale evenings, consider waterproof leather boots or stylish flats.

3. **Headwear Isn't Just for Royalty**:
    - A broad-brimmed hat keeps raindrops and rays at bay during your Hyde Park adventures.
    - Woolly beanies? They're perfect for brisk Jack-the-Ripper walking tours (and they'll keep your ears toasty)
.
4. **Choose the Right Bag**:
    - In a city where you'll carry everything from rain gear to souvenirs, pick a bag with multiple compartments.
    - Opt for a material that can withstand the elements—because British weather loves surprises
.

Remember, adapting to a new culture is an adventure! Whether you're savoring a hearty pie or braving a sudden shower, embrace it all.

British desserts have a delightful mix of tradition, nostalgia, and comforting flavors. Let's explore some popular ones that you'll want to savor:

1. **Scottish Shortbread**:
    - This buttery delight traces its roots back to Scotland. It's believed to have been enjoyed since the Middle

Ages and was even favored by Mary Queen of Scots. The secret to perfect shortbread? Letting the dough chill!

2. **Old English Trifle**:
   - A classic trifle is a layered masterpiece. Picture sponge cake, custard, jelly, whipped cream, and berries all coming together. It's been a favorite in Britain for over 300 years.

3. **Mincemeat Pie**:
   - Don't be fooled by the name! Mincemeat pies no longer contain actual meat. Instead, they're filled with a sweet mixture of apples, raisins, spices, and sometimes nuts. Perfect for the holiday season or any cool day.

4. **Madeira Cake**:
   - Named after Madeira wine, this cake is similar to a pound cake. It's often flavored with lemon and pairs wonderfully with tea or other sweet liqueurs.

5. **Steamed Plum Pudding (Figgy Pudding)**:

- Plum pudding has quite the history! Originally savory in the 14th century, it transformed into a dessert. These days, it's made with brown sugar, currants, alcohol, and spices. Yes, it's the same figgy pudding we sing about at Christmas!
6.
7. **Jammy Dodgers**:
    - These iconic biscuits (cookies) are everywhere in the UK. Tender buttery cookies sandwiched with jam—what's not to love? Finish them off with a dusting of confectioners' sugar.

8. **Battenberg Cake**:
    - Seen on "The Great British Baking Show," Battenberg cake features two shades of sponge cake with a jam filling, all wrapped in marzipan. It's fit for royalty!

And that's just the beginning! British desserts are a delightful journey through time and taste. So, which one will you try first?

8 EMOTIONAL RESILIENCE

Let's explore emotional resilience, starting with homesickness and then diving into cultural identity.

Coping with Homesickness:

Homesickness is a common experience, especially when you're adjusting to a new environment. Here are some strategies to help you navigate those feelings:

1. **Acknowledge Your Feelings**:
    - It's okay to miss home! Acknowledge your emotions without judgment. Homesickness is a sign that you have meaningful connections to your past.
    - Take time to reflect on what you miss most—whether it's family,

familiar places, or certain routines.

2. **Stay Connected**:
   - Regularly communicate with loved ones back home. Video calls, messages, and even old-fashioned letters can bridge the distance.
   - Share your experiences with them and let them be part of your new journey.

3. **Create Familiar Rituals**:
   - Establish routines that remind you of home. Maybe it's brewing a cup of tea just like your grandmother used to make or listening to familiar music.
   - These small rituals provide comfort and continuity.

4. **Explore Your New Environment**:
   - While missing home, also explore your current surroundings. Discover local parks, cafes, and hidden gems.
   - Each new place has its own magic waiting to be uncovered.

5. **Make New Connections**:
   - Cultivate friendships and social connections. Attend local events,

join clubs, or participate in group activities.
- Shared experiences create bonds and ease feelings of isolation.

6. **Self-Care**:
   - Prioritize self-care. Get enough rest, eat well, and engage in activities that bring you joy.
   - Exercise, mindfulness, and hobbies can boost your mood.

Remember, homesickness is a natural part of adjusting to change. Over time, it tends to lessen as you build new memories and connections. You're not alone in feeling this way!

Embracing Cultural Identity:

1. **Celebrate Your Heritage**:
   - Hold onto your cultural roots. Cook traditional dishes, listen to familiar music, and share stories from your background.
   - These practices anchor you and remind you of who you are.

2. **Learn About Local Culture**:
   - While embracing your own heritage, also explore the culture around you.

Attend local events, festivals, and exhibitions.
- The UK hosts a rich tapestry of cultural celebrations throughout the year!

Some notable UK festivals include:

- **Edinburgh Fringe Festival**: A vibrant celebration of performing arts held in August.
- **Glyndebourne Festival**: World-class classical music performances set against the stunning South Downs countryside.
- **Notting Hill Carnival**: A colorful Caribbean-inspired street festival in London.
- **Hay Festival**: A literary extravaganza featuring renowned authors and artists in Wales.

3. **Be Curious and Open-Minded**:
    - Engage with people from diverse backgrounds. Ask questions, listen, and learn.
    - Appreciate the richness that cultural diversity brings.

Remember, your cultural identity is a mosaic—a beautiful blend of where you come from and where you're headed. Enjoy the journey!

British traditions and customs are a fascinating blend of history, culture, and regional diversity. Let's explore some of the delightful traditions that make the UK unique:

1. **Afternoon Tea**:
    - Ah, the quintessential British ritual! Picture delicate china cups, freshly brewed tea, and tiers of scones, finger sandwiches, and pastries. Afternoon tea is a delightful way to pause and indulge.

2. **Changing of the Guard at Buckingham Palace**:
    - Head to Buckingham Palace in London to witness this iconic ceremony. The guards, resplendent in their red tunics and bearskin hats, perform a precise drill as they change shifts. It's a royal spectacle!

3. **Pantomime (Panto)**:
    - Panto season is a magical time around Christmas. These theatrical

productions combine fairy tales, slapstick humor, cross-dressing, and audience participation. Oh yes, they do!

4. **Guy Fawkes Night (Bonfire Night)**:
   - On November 5th, Brits commemorate the foiled Gunpowder Plot of 1605. Expect bonfires, fireworks, and effigies of Guy Fawkes burning merrily.

5. **Morris Dancing**:
   - Picture bells, ribbons, and sticks. Morris dancers perform lively, rhythmic routines at village fetes and summer festivals. It's a centuries-old tradition that still brings smiles.

6. **May Day Celebrations**:
   - Maypole dancing, flower crowns, and the arrival of spring—May Day festivities are a joyous affair. Villages decked in greenery and flowers celebrate the changing seasons.

7. **Christmas Crackers**:
   - At Christmas dinner, everyone pulls a cracker—a colorful paper tube

filled with a joke, a paper crown, and a tiny toy. The resulting "pop" adds to the festive cheer.

8. **Highland Games (Scotland)**:
    - Kilts, bagpipes, and feats of strength! The Highland Games feature caber tossing, hammer throwing, and tug-of-war. It's a celebration of Scottish heritage.

9. **Royal Ascot**:
    - Ladies in extravagant hats, gentlemen in top hats, and thoroughbred horse racing—it's all part of the Royal Ascot, a prestigious event attended by the Queen herself.

10. **Wassailing**:
    - In cider-producing regions, wassailing involves singing, dancing, and toasting apple trees to ensure a good harvest. It's a merry way to encourage fruitfulness!

Remember, these traditions vary across the UK—from the rolling hills of Scotland to the bustling streets of London. Each one adds to the rich tapestry of British life!

9 DRIVING AND TRANSPORT

Let's delve into driving and transportation in the UK. Whether you're hitting the road or hopping on public transport, I've got you covered!

Driving License in the UK:

1. **Provisional Driving License**:
   - If you're new to driving in the UK, start by applying for a provisional (learner's) driving license. You can do this online through the official GOV.UK website.
   - To apply, you'll need to:
     - Be able to read a number plate from 20 meters away.
     - Provide a legitimate form of ID (usually a passport).
     - List your addresses for the

past three years.

2. **Theory Test and Practical Driving Test**:
   o Once you have your provisional license, it's time to prepare for the journey ahead:
     - Book and pass your theory test. This assesses your knowledge of road rules, signs, and safe driving practices.
     - Sign up for driving lessons to build your skills.
     - Finally, book and pass your practical driving test. Show off those parallel parking skills!

3. **Full Driving License**:
   o After passing your practical test, you'll receive a driving test pass certificate.
   o Fill out form D1 (the "application for a driving license") and sign the declaration.
   o Include original documents confirming your identity.
   o Voilà! You'll soon have your full UK driving license.

Road Rules and Traffic Signs:
- The UK follows a comprehensive system of traffic signs. While The Highway Code provides many examples, you can find a detailed explanation in the Department's booklet called "Know Your Traffic Signs." It covers everything from prohibitive signs (with red circles) to positive instructions (with blue circles).
- Keep an eye out for bilingual signs in Wales, which include both Welsh and English versions of place names.
- If you're curious about specific signs or need more information, feel free to ask!

Public Transport:

1. **Buses and Coaches**:
    - Local buses connect towns, cities, and rural areas. They're a convenient way to explore.
    - Coaches (long-distance buses) operate between major cities and even cross-country. They're comfortable and often cost-effective.
2. **Trains**:
    - The UK has an extensive rail network. Trains connect cities,

towns, and scenic routes.
- London's Underground (the Tube) is iconic and efficient. It's the heartbeat of the capital.
3. **Airports**:
     - Major airports are well-connected to cities via public transport. London alone has six airports, with Heathrow and London City directly linked to the Tube network.
4. **Taxis and Ride-Sharing**:
     - Taxis are available in most cities. Look for licensed black cabs or use ride-sharing apps.
     - Uber operates in many UK cities.

Remember, whether you're behind the wheel or hopping on a train, enjoy the journey and stay safe!

Let's explore the speed limits in the UK. Whether you're cruising through picturesque countryside or navigating city streets, knowing the limits is essential for safe driving.

Here's a breakdown of the key speed limits:

1. **Built-Up Areas (Urban Roads)**:
     - In most built-up areas (where you'll find houses, shops, and schools), the

speed limit is **30 miles per hour (48 km/h)**. This applies to cars, motorcycles, car-derived vans, and dual-purpose vehicles.
- However, in **Wales**, the limit is **20 miles per hour (32 km/h)** within built-up areas.

2. **Single Carriageways (Non-Dual Carriageways)**:
    - On single carriageways (roads with one lane in each direction), the speed limit for cars, motorcycles, and similar vehicles is **60 miles per hour (96 km/h)**.
    - If you're towing a caravan or trailer, the limit drops to **50 miles per hour (80 km/h)**.

3. **Dual Carriageways and Motorways**:
    - On dual carriageways (roads with two lanes in each direction, separated by a central reservation), the speed limit for cars and motorcycles is **70 miles per hour (112 km/h)**.
    - Motorhomes (up to 3.05 tonnes unladen weight) can also travel at this speed on dual carriageways.
    - When towing a caravan or trailer,

the limit reduces to **60 miles per hour (96 km/h)**.
- On motorways (the high-speed highways), the maximum speed for cars, motorcycles, and motorhomes is also **70 miles per hour (112 km/h)**.

4. **Goods Vehicles and Buses**:
    - Goods vehicles (up to 7.5 tonnes maximum laden weight) follow the same limits as cars on single carriageways and dual carriageways.
    - However, if they're articulated or towing a trailer, the limit drops to **60 miles per hour (96 km/h)**.
    - In Scotland, goods vehicles (over 7.5 tonnes) have a lower limit of **40 miles per hour (64 km/h)** on single carriageways.

5. **Vans and Car-Derived Vans**:
    - Most vans have a lower speed limit than cars. They must follow the speed limits for goods vehicles of the same weight.
    - However, vans under 2 tonnes laden weight are considered "car-derived vans" and have the same speed limits as cars.

6. **Locally Set Speed Limits**:
    - Local councils can set their own speed limits in specific areas. These limits must be clearly signed.

Remember, these limits are the absolute maximum—always adjust your speed based on road conditions, visibility, and traffic. Safety first!

10 FINANCE AND BENEFITS

Let's dive into financial literacy, specifically focusing on banking, taxes, and how to navigate them in the UK.

Opening a UK Bank Account:

1. UK Bank Account for US Citizens:
- As a US citizen, you can indeed open a UK bank account. The process varies based on whether you're a UK resident or a non-resident.
- If you're already a UK resident, opening an account online is straightforward. You'll need acceptable proof of identity and details of your UK address.
- For newcomers without traditional UK

proof of address, online and digital providers (like Wise or Revolut) offer more flexible verification processes. They can use your US proof of identity and address to set up an account before your arrival in the UK.

- Here's a step-by-step guide:

    o **Choose the Bank and Account**: Research and select a bank that suits your needs.
    o **Download the Provider App or Visit Their Website**: Apply online through the app or desktop site.
    o **Provide Necessary Information**: You'll need to verify your identity and provide details about your UK address.
    o **Submit Your Application**: Follow the instructions provided by the bank or provider.

2. Tax Regulations and Filing Requirements:
- **Income Tax in the UK**:
    o Income Tax is levied on various types of income, including earnings from employment, self-employment, state benefits, pensions, rental income, and interest on savings.

- However, there are exemptions—for instance, the first £1,000 of income from self-employment or property rental.
- Most people in the UK have a Personal Allowance of tax-free income, which reduces the amount of tax they pay.
- If you qualify, there are additional tax reliefs available.

- **Non-Residents and UK Tax Returns**:
  - If you're a non-resident, you may need to file a UK tax return if you have UK income (such as employment, business, rental, or investment income) or UK assets (like property or shares).
  - Some non-residents also maintain a UK bank account, which may be subject to tax reporting requirements.
  - Ensure accuracy when filing your tax returns, and consider seeking professional advice if needed.

Remember, understanding the UK's financial landscape is essential for a smooth transition. Whether you're setting up your bank account or navigating tax obligations, take it step by step.

National Insurance contributions (NICs) play a crucial role in the UK's tax system. Let's dive into the details:

1. **What Are National Insurance Contributions (NICs)?**
    - NICs are essentially taxes paid by both employees and employers. These contributions fund various government benefits programs, including:
        - **Universal Health Care**: Supporting the National Health Service (NHS), which provides healthcare services to residents.
        - **Public Pension Program**: Ensuring that individuals receive a state pension when they reach retirement age.
        - **Unemployment Benefits**: Providing financial support to those who are temporarily out of work.

2. **Who Pays NICs?**
    - Employees: If you're 16 or older and earn over £242 per week from one job, you're required to pay NICs.

- Self-Employed Individuals: If you're self-employed and your annual profit exceeds £12,570, NICs apply.
- Employers: Employers also contribute NICs based on the earnings of their employees.

3. **Thresholds and Exemptions**:
   - Up to a certain threshold, earnings are exempt from NICs. For instance:
     - If you're over the state pension age (even if you're still working), you don't pay NICs.
     - Employees earning between £123 and £242 per week (or self-employed individuals with profits of £6,725 or more per year) may not pay NICs but could still qualify for benefits and the state pension.

4. **Voluntary Contributions**:
   - Sometimes, gaps occur in your NICs record (e.g., due to periods of unemployment or low earnings). In such cases, you can make voluntary contributions to protect your entitlement to benefits and the state

pension.
   o

Remember, NICs are an essential part of the UK's social safety net, ensuring that everyone contributes toward vital services and support. If you have specific questions about your own situation, it's a good idea to seek professional advice.

Child Benefit is an essential support provided by the UK government to parents. Let's dive into how it works:

1. **Eligibility and Claiming**:
     - You can claim Child Benefit if you're responsible for a child who is:
         - Under 16 years old.
         - Under 20 years old if they're in approved education or training.
     - Only one person can claim Child Benefit for a child, but there's no limit to how many children you can claim for.

2. **What You Get**:
     - Child Benefit is paid at a weekly rate:
         - £20.70 for the first child.
         - £13.70 for each additional child.

- By claiming Child Benefit, you receive:
  - **An Allowance**: This allowance is paid directly to you every 4 weeks.
  - **National Insurance Credits**: These credits count toward your State Pension, ensuring you don't have gaps in your National Insurance record.
  - **National Insurance Number for Your Child**: Your child will receive a National Insurance number without needing to apply separately. They usually get it shortly before turning.

3. **High-Income Child Benefit Charge**:
   - If you or your partner earns more than £60,000 a year before tax, you can still claim Child Benefit.
   - However, there's a catch: You'll have to pay back some (or all) of your Child Benefit in the form of extra Income Tax.
   - Specifically:
     - For every £200 you earn above £60,000, you'll need to pay back 1% of the maximum

Child Benefit amount you're entitled to.
- At £80,000 a year, the charge equals 100% of your entitlement, effectively canceling out the benefit.

Remember, claiming Child Benefit not only provides financial support but also helps protect your State Pension.

Visit Arthurcrandon.co.uk for More Titles

Retirement to the Philippines
K1 Fiance visa to the U.S. – Fast Track
Secrets to buying Condos in the Philippines
Buying Land in the Philippines
Annulment in the Philippines
Breaking free from a bad marriage
Get a visit visa to America First time
Marriage in the Philippines
Get a visit visa to the United Kingdom
Ghosts, Spectres, and folklore in the Philippines
Retiring to Spain – a Comprehensive Guide
Spousal Visa to America
Spousal visa to the United Kingdom
Working in the UK.
Working in the US.

ABOUT THE AUTHOR

Arthur Crandon is a retired lawyer and a prolific writer. He is British and grew up in a rural community in Somerset. He has lived in England, Wales, Hong Kong and the Philippines and now spends most of his time in the Philippines with his Visayan wife and their son.

He loves to hear from anyone who has anything to do with the Philippines – you can email him anytime on:

ac@arthurcrandon.co.uk

www.ingramcontent.com/pod-product-compliance
Lightning Source LLC
Chambersburg PA
CBHW070352230526
45471CB00006B/2528